Anna's Silent World

by Bernard Wolf

HarperCollins*Publishers*

ACKNOWLEDGMENTS

The author wishes to express his gratitude to the following persons for their generous assistance and support during the preparation of this book:

Dorothy Briley (whose perceptive collaboration in preparing the text was invaluable), Jean Krulis and Carlos Crosbie of J. B. Lippincott Company; Manuel M. Cuenca, administrator of the New York League for the Hard of Hearing, New York City; Jane R. Madell, Ph.D., director of audiology services, and Karen Webb, former speech pathologist, the New York League for the Hard of Hearing; Katherine Taylor, principal, St. Luke's School, New York City; Gay Gross, former teacher, St. Luke's School; Laurie Abramson, dance instructor; Margaret Pardo of New York City; and once again Mike Levins, who prepared the beautiful photographic prints for this book. To Anna and all the special people in her family, the author can only say, "Thank you very much!" May this book bring you pleasure in the years to come.

U.S. Library of Congress Cataloging in Publication Data
Wolf, Bernard.   Anna's silent world.
SUMMARY: Describes special training and equipment used to help a deaf youngster talk, read, and write.   1. Children, Deaf—Juvenile literature. 2. Deaf—Means of communication—Juvenile literature. 3. New York League for the Hard of Hearing. [1. Deaf. 2. Physically handicapped] I. Title.
HV2561.N7W64   371.9'12   76-52943
ISBN 0-397-31739-5
ISBN 0-397-32503-7 (lib. bdg.)

FOR DOROTHY BRILEY
who has mastered
the art of
listening

This is Anna. She lives in New York City with her mother and father, her brother Danny and her sister Suzi. She has an older, married, sister April.

Most mornings when Anna wakes up the first thing she sees is Tycho. When Anna touches him she can feel his rumbling purr.

Without special help Anna cannot hear the sound of Tycho's purr or her dog Homer's bark or her brother's violin. Anna was born deaf.

But Anna is learning to talk and to read and write the way people around her do. Her family, close friends and the boys and girls she goes to school with all have normal hearing. The world that is silent for Anna is the same one that is full of sound for almost everyone she knows.

She receives special training to overcome her deafness at the New York League for the Hard of Hearing. Here, Dr. Jane R. Madell gives Anna her yearly audiological evaluation. This is a test to see if there have been any changes in her ability to hear. Dr. Madell describes Anna as "a child with a profound hearing loss." This means that Anna can hear almost nothing. However, like most deaf people, Anna can hear some sounds. At the League she is learning to use what little hearing she has.

The loudness of sound is measured in decibels: One decibel is very soft and the numbers go up as the sound gets louder. Most people can hear when a sound is between 1 and 25 decibels. A sound must be very loud—at least 90 decibels—before Anna can hear when she is not wearing her hearing aids. With the aids she hears some sounds at 55 decibels.

Anna is holding a peg in her hand ready to place it in a hole on the board when she hears an amplified tone through the earphones. This test helps Dr. Madell choose the best kind of hearing aids for Anna to use.

When Anna is finished with Dr. Madell, she goes to her regular therapy session with speech pathologist Karen Webb. Anna works with Miss Webb for an hour twice a week. Anna is using earphones that are connected to a special amplifier that makes sounds spoken into a microphone very loud.

Anna watches and listens to Miss Webb very carefully. She then repeats what she hears, trying to use the same movements of tongue, mouth, face and body that Miss Webb uses.

14

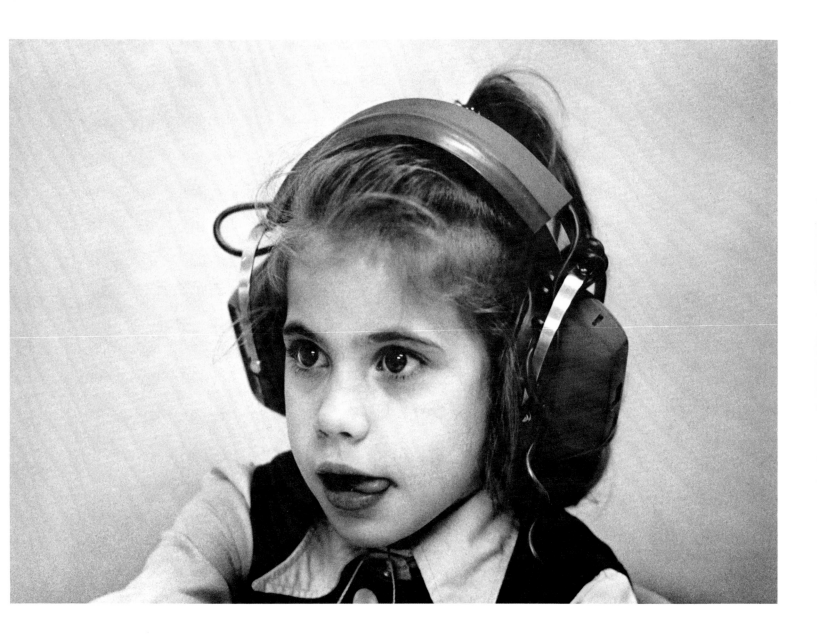

Learning how to talk and to lip-read is the hardest part of Anna's therapy. Even with amplification she can hear only parts of the words spoken to her.

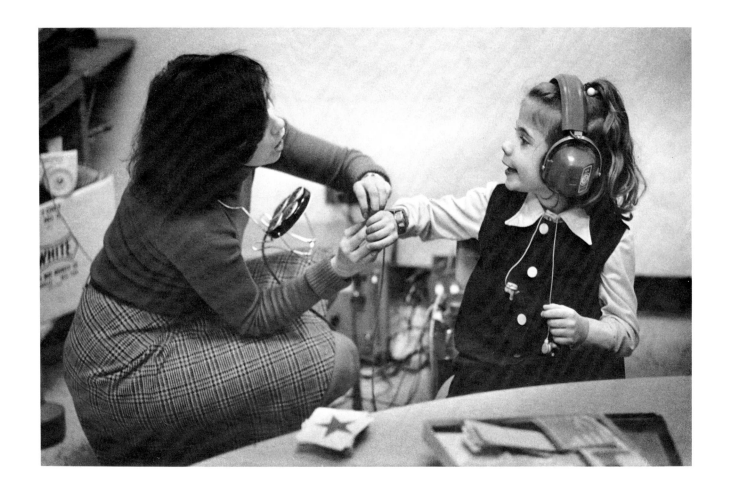

We hear because sound makes our ear drums vibrate and the auditory nerves carry sound sensations to the brain. Anna's auditory nerves do not work as they should. The vibrator Miss Webb is placing on Anna's wrist is also connected to the amplifier. When she speaks into the microphone sound is conducted through the bones of Anna's wrist and arm. This reinforces what she hears through the earphones and helps Anna learn to use her whole body to distinguish sounds.

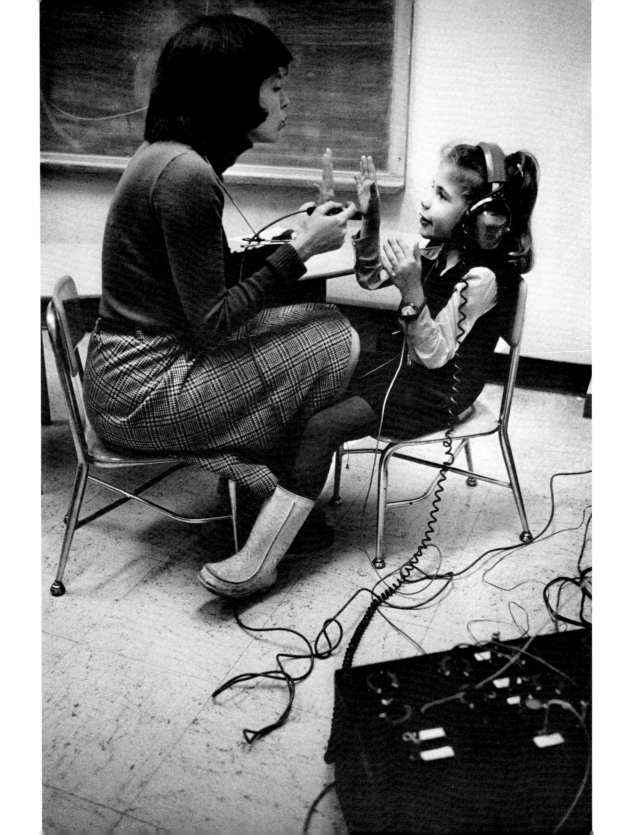

It is especially important for Anna to learn to pronounce words correctly so that other people can understand what she says. Today, using only the hearing aids she wears every day, Anna is practicing words that have the "t" (tuh) sound at the beginning, middle or end. She spins the dial and makes a sentence using the name of the object that the dial points to.

Anna has been working with people at the New York League for the Hard of Hearing since she was two years old. The League believes that the best way to help the deaf is to teach them how to communicate by listening and speaking the way people with normal hearing do.

Anna uses what she learns all the time. She is in first grade at St. Luke's School near her home. For her, school is a happy place where she loves to find out about new things.

In class Anna sits up front and concentrates all her attention
on the story her teacher is reading.

22

She watches Miss Gross's lips and body language and the pictures in the book.

After reading class it's time for recess on the playground. Even though it's a cold December day, Anna chooses to sit on the swings instead of running and playing with her classmates.

At lunchtime Anna munches her peanut butter and jelly sandwich and concentrates on what a classmate across the table is telling her.

24

She stops by the library on her way back to the classroom. She's only halfway through the book when it's time for a geography lesson. Miss Gross points out the spot on the globe where New York City is located.

The rest of the afternoon passes quickly. First she has an arithmetic lesson, and finally she does an exercise in her writing workbook.

Once a week Anna attends a ballet class taught by Laurie Abramson.

Miss Abramson shows Anna how to improve her body position, and the music begins.

Anna can sense the basic rhythms of the music and keep time with them. Today the music is from *The Nutcracker* because Christmas is only a few days away.

At first Anna was self-conscious about the way her body aids show through her leotard, but the pleasure of dancing quickly helped her overcome that feeling.

Saturday is one of Anna's favorite days of the week. Her father is home all day. This morning he shows Anna and Danny microscopic animals that live in a drop of water.

This particular Saturday is all the more exciting because there are only a few more days until Christmas. Anna's best friend Margaret Pardo has come to spend the afternoon. Everybody else is busy shopping or wrapping presents, and at first Anna and Margaret keep very quiet drawing and writing stories.

34

But sitting still is hard to keep up for very long.

Even Tycho has to have something to say about all the excitement in the air.

"Come catch me!" yells Anna. And with a quick leap, Tycho almost does.

But Margaret hasn't understood Anna clearly. Anna's mother comes into the room just as Anna is trying to repeat herself.

"Sometimes it's hard for me to figure out what Anna is saying."

"That's because Anna is still learning how to speak clearly," Anna's mother tells her. "Deaf children need to hear a word hundreds of times before they can use it the way you and I do. Even with her hearing aids, Anna hears much less than you do. It will take her longer to speak clearly, but she'll catch up. By the time the two of you are in high school, her speech will be almost like anyone else's."

"Well, most of the time I know what she's saying," Margaret says. "The thing is, if she can't hear me, how does she know what *I'm* saying?"

"Anna has to look at you and read your lips to hear, and her hearing aids help. Let me show you."

Anna's mother shows Margaret the two amplifiers that Anna wears strapped to her chest under her shirt. The amplifiers are powered by batteries and a wire runs from each of them to the

earpieces. When the amplifiers are turned on, they make sounds louder and Anna can hear more than she can without them.

Anna lets Margaret listen with one of her hearing aids. They tell each other Christmas secrets.

Anna and her family look forward to the holidays the way most families do. Christmas is a special time which brings them together. On Christmas Eve they decorate a tree and sing carols and enjoy one another's company.

Anna trims the tree with tinsel and teases Suzi to tell her what is in the long skinny box under the tree with her name on it.

When the last present is wrapped and the last ornament is on the tree, Anna's father and Homer relax with Christmas eggnog. On Christmas morning there's something under the tree for everyone. April and her husband have come to take part in opening presents. There are many exclamations of "Oh, that's just

what I wanted!" and "You shouldn't have!" Anna admires her mother's set of giant coffee mugs and Homer gives a "Woof" of approval to Suzi's new shoulder bag. Christmas morning is a noisy, happy time.

And Anna's favorite present is a recorder. Now she can add her own music to the sounds of her silent world.

48